Talking about
Death

Karen Bryant-Mole

RAINTREE
STECK-VAUGHN
PUBLISHERS
A Steck-Vaughn Company

Austin, Texas

Titles in the series

Talking about

Alcohol   **Disability**

Bullying   **Drugs**

Death   **Family Breakup**

Published by Raintree Steck-Vaughn Publishers,
an imprint of Steck-Vaughn Company

Library of Congress Cataloging-in-Publication Data
Bryant-Mole, Karen.
Talking about death / Karen Bryant-Mole.
   p.   cm.—(Talking about)
   Includes bibliographical references and index.
   Summary: Focuses on death as part of a natural cycle
   and as part of the entire process of life; also discusses
   common responses to death.
   ISBN 0-8172-5536-2
   1. Death—Juvenile literature.
   [1. Death.]
   I. Title. II. Series.
   BD444.B755   1999
   155.9'37—dc21   98-19781

96624

Printed in Italy. Bound in the United States.
1 2 3 4 5 6 7 8 9 0 03 02 01 00 99

Picture acknowledgments
The publishers would like to thank the following for allowing their pictures to be produced in this book: Martyn F. Chillmaid *cover*, *title page*, *contents page*, 19, 22, 23, 24, 25, 26; Bruce Coleman Ltd/Werner Layer 5 (top), /Mr J. Brackenburg 5 (bottom), /Kim Taylor 6, /Jane Burton 8, 9 (both), /Hans Reinhard 14; Eye Ubiquitous/Skjold 18; Getty Images'/Nicole Katano 4, /Lori Adamski Peek 10, /Don Smetzer 11, /Andrew Sacks 13, /Julian Calder 15, /Donald C. Johnson/The Stockmarket 16, /Jon Riley 20, /Peter Correz 21, /Peter Cade 27 (top); The Hutchison Library 17 (bottom); Impact/Norman Lomax 17 (top), /Bruce Stephens 27 (bottom); Wayland Publishers Ltd 12.

Contents

I'm Alive

To understand what death means, we first of all have to understand what being alive means.

This giraffe is alive.
So is this butterfly.

You are alive, too. Like
the butterfly and the giraffe, you
can breathe, eat, move, and grow.

Dying

When people or animals die, the life goes out of their bodies. This bird has died because of the cold weather. The bird is dead. Its body is still there, but it has no life.

When someone, or something, dies you
might think of their body as being like
an empty house where someone used to
live.

Lives

All living things have lives that follow patterns.

These puppies have just been born. They are at the beginning of their lives.

Over the next few months they will grow bigger and stronger.

By the time they are a year old these puppies will be fully grown. They will be able to have puppies of their own.

Growing Old

A fully grown living thing is known as an adult.

Young adults usually have bodies that are fit and healthy. They can run fast and have lots of energy.

As adults get older, they start to slow down, and their bodies begin to wear out.

Death

Death comes at the end of every life.
We are born, we live our lives, and
we die.

People die when something happens to
their bodies that means it doesn't work.

Some bodies may have been damaged in an accident. Some may have been damaged through illness or disease. And some may just wear out through old age.

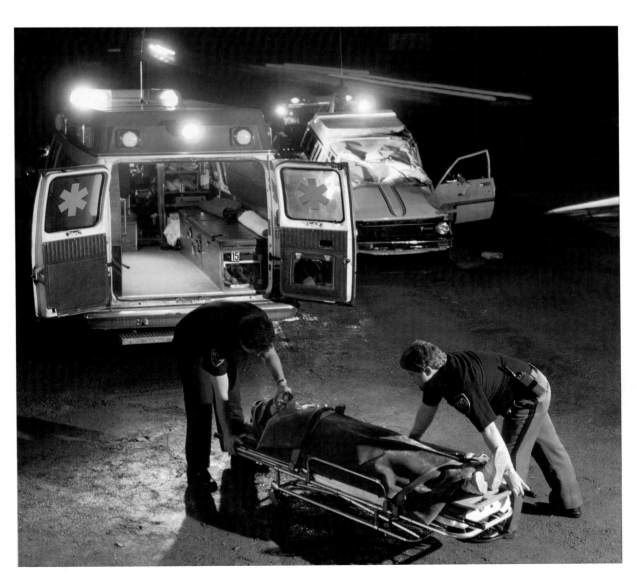

Long Lives, Short Lives

Different living things live for different lengths of time. This hamster will probably live for two to three years.

People are usually expected to live to about 75. A few people live more than 100 years.

Just as some people live longer, some people have much shorter lives.

People who are very seriously ill or who have been in a bad accident can die, no matter what their age.

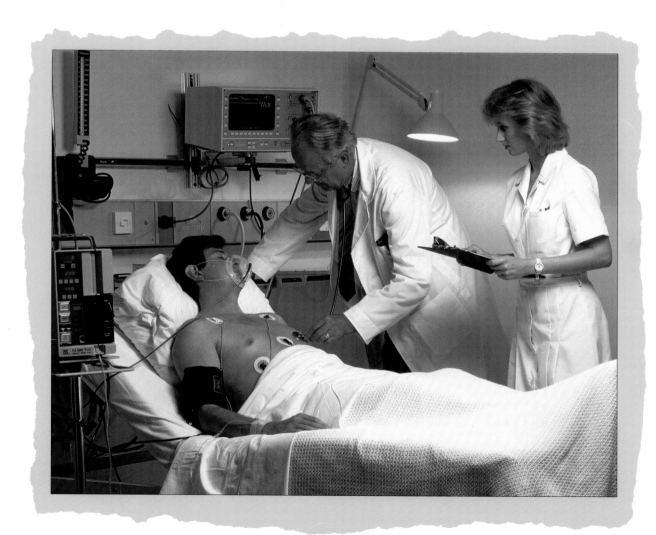

Funerals

After someone has died, there is usually a funeral. A funeral is a special ceremony. It is often held in a religious building, such as a church or a synagogue.

The funeral is a
chance for all the
people who cared
about the person
who has died to
come together.
It is a way of
saying good-bye to
the person who
has died.

Feeling Sad

When someone dies, people who knew
that person often feel sad.

People often feel sad when a pet dies, too.
Lucy cried and cried when her cat died.

Feeling sad is a good thing. It shows that
you really loved and cared for the person
or pet who died.

Missing Someone

If someone we care about goes away and we know we may not see them again, we feel sad and miss them.

If someone or something that you care about dies, you know you will not see them again and will probably miss them even more.

You might particularly miss them at special times when you used to be together.

Amy used to walk her dog in the park.
After her dog died, she missed him
very much whenever she went there
without him.

Feeling Angry

People sometimes feel cross or angry when someone, or something, dies.

They might feel angry because they don't think it is fair that the person they loved has died.

Sam felt mad at himself for not
telling his grandmother
how much he loved her.

But Sam's grandmother probably
understood that he loved her, even
though he might not have said so.

Helping

It can be difficult to understand what it must feel like when someone you love dies.

Leila's friend Jack was very upset when his grandfather died. He felt sad and lonely.

Leila tried to be especially kind and thoughtful. It helped Jack to know that he had a good friend like Leila.

Remembering

It can take a long time to get over the death of someone or something you love.

Getting over a death doesn't mean forgetting. It just means that you start to feel less upset.

Instead, you
may be able
to remember
all the good
times you
had together.

Notes for Parents and Teachers

This book can be used in two ways. It can serve as an introduction to the sensitive topic of death. It can also be used to help and support children who have recently experienced personal bereavement. The approach is deliberately secular, allowing you, as parents and teachers, to introduce any spiritual aspects you may wish, according to your own religious beliefs. The book explains the biological process of life and death, encouraging children to understand death as part of a natural cycle. It also deals with responses to death.

Children vary enormously in their reaction to death. Often the loss of a loved family pet will have a more profound effect than the death of a grandparent or other family member who was not such a regular feature of the child's life. Not only will the response be dependent on the child's relationship with the person or, perhaps, pet who has died, but on the child's age and character, too. Young children, in particular, live in a very self-centered world, and if the death has no

immediate effect on their everyday lives, they may show little emotion. Parents sometimes feel hurt by this reaction, fearing that their child is uncaring or unfeeling. But emotions cannot and should not be forced on people. In some ways perhaps it is better to be grateful that your child is not having to experience the grief that others around him or her may be feeling.

Other children may react to death with great distress. Sometimes this distress is displayed obviously, through tears and sadness, but sometimes it may be displayed as naughtiness, anger, or even a withdrawing into oneself. As adults, one of the most important things you can do for bereaved children is simply to be there for them. Talking is an important part of the grieving process. Let the child know that you are there when, and if, he or she wants to talk.

Glossary

Adult A fully grown person or animal.

Ceremony A set of words and actions that are said and performed the same way each time, to mark an important event.

Church A building where people who follow the Christian religion go.

Disease An illness that can be passed on from one person to another.

Energy The strength to do things.

Fit In a healthy condition.

Funeral A special ceremony, held when someone dies.

Pattern Something that happens in the same way over and over again.

Books to Read

Palmer, Pat. *"I Wish I Could Hold Your Hand:" A Child's Guide to Grief and Loss.* Obispo, CA: Impact Publishers, 1994.

Rothman, Juliet C. *A Birthday Present for Daniel: A Child's Story of Loss.* Amherst, NY: Prometheus Books, 1996.

Spelman, Cornelia. *After Charlotte's Mom Died.* Morton Grove, IL: Albert Whitman, 1996.

Index

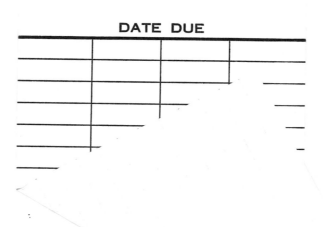

DATE DUE